Original title:
The Wise Path to Love

Copyright © 2024 Book Fairy Publishing
All rights reserved.

Author: Claudia Kuma
ISBN HARDBACK: 978-9916-87-345-8
ISBN PAPERBACK: 978-9916-87-346-5
ISBN EBOOK: 978-9916-87-347-2

The Quill and the Heart

In silence, the quill does dance,
Stories born from a fleeting glance.
Ink spills dreams upon the page,
With each stroke, we turn the wage.

A heart that beats with every line,
Words like whispers, pure and divine.
Emotions flow with ink so deep,
In quiet moments, secrets keep.

The quill remembers, never forgets,
In every word, the heart besets.
Legacy written in the night,
As passion ignites the soul's light.

So let us write, let our thoughts soar,
With quill in hand, we dare to explore.
In stories shared, we find our way,
The quill and the heart, in endless play.

Garden of Wishes and Whispers

In a garden where dreams take flight,
Wishes bloom in the soft moonlight.
Petals whisper secrets of old,
In colors vivid, stories unfold.

Every flower holds a sweet prayer,
Hopes entwined in the fragrant air.
With each breeze, a promise flows,
In the hush, where the twilight glows.

Paths of ivy draw us near,
To listen closely, hearts sincere.
Among the blooms, love's gentle sigh,
As stars blink softly in the sky.

In this garden, our spirits blend,
Wishes granted, as fears suspend.
With whispers carried on the breeze,
In this haven, our souls find peace.

Unraveled Secrets of the Heart

In whispers soft, our stories weave,
Beneath the stars, secrets we leave.
Each gaze exchanged, a pact profound,
In silence shared, love's voice is found.

The depths we dive, with courage bold,
Nurturing dreams, in warmth enfold.
Unraveled threads, we hold so tight,
Together we craft, both day and night.

The Starry Voyage of Togetherness

Beneath the glow of twinkling lights,
We sail through time, on endless flights.
With hands entwined, we chart our course,
In the night's embrace, we find our source.

Together, facing every storm,
In laughter's echo, hearts keep warm.
Through constellations, our love will soar,
In every journey, we seek for more.

Sunsets in Each Other's Arms

As daylight fades, colors bright blend,
In silent moments, both heart and friend.
Wrapped in whispers, we find our peace,
In sunsets' glow, our worries cease.

Each shadow dances in soft retreat,
The world slows down, as time feels sweet.
In each other's arms, dreams take flight,
Forever anchored in love's soft light.

Traces of Laughter in the Air

In every chuckle, memories bloom,
In joyful echoes, we fill the room.
With playful hearts, we chase the sun,
In laughter's cradle, we are one.

Through days we wander, with smiles aglow,
Each playful jest, a gentle flow.
In the air, love's melody sings,
Forever cherished, in simple things.

Threads of Fate and Feeling

In the loom of life's design,
Threads entwine, a pattern fine.
With each tug, the fate does turn,
In silent whispers, hearts will yearn.

Moments pass like fleeting light,
Binding souls, in day and night.
A tapestry of joy and pain,
In every stitch, love's sweet refrain.

Scribe of Unspoken Promises

Beneath the stars, the silence breathes,
A story hidden, in trust it weaves.
Words unspoken linger near,
In the heart's soft echo, crystal clear.

Ink of dreams upon the page,
Time will turn, and thoughts engage.
A promise kept, a bond so tight,
In whispered hopes, we find our light.

Lanterns Along a Serene Trail

Glow of lanterns in the night,
Guiding paths, a warm delight.
Stars above and whispers low,
In the stillness, love will flow.

Each step brings a world anew,
A tranquil heart, where dreams break through.
Underneath the moon's soft gaze,
In the calm, we seek our ways.

The Dance of Serendipity

In moments bright, where chance aligns,
A twist of fate, in gentle signs.
Two souls collide, with laughter's grace,
In serendipity's sweet embrace.

Life's rhythm sways, a song we share,
With every glance, a spark, a flare.
The dance unfolds, so wild, so free,
In this moment, just you and me.

Serene Streams of Affection

Through gentle whispers, soft and clear,
Love flows like water, free of fear.
In tranquil moments, hearts align,
Two souls entwined, a love divine.

Beneath the willow, shadows play,
Reminding us of love's sweet sway.
Together we wander, hand in hand,
In the serene glow of quiet land.

Fragments of Forever

Every glance a piece of time,
A treasure found in rhythm and rhyme.
Memories linger, like soft sighs,
In the canvas that never dies.

Each heartbeat echoes, faint yet clear,
In this dance of love held near.
Fragments woven, thread by thread,
In a tapestry of words unsaid.

Whirlwind of Shared Moments

Life spins swiftly, a vibrant dance,
In every smile, we find romance.
Together we navigate the storm,
In each embrace, we feel the warm.

Laughter bubbles, joy takes flight,
In stolen glances, hearts ignite.
Through every twist, our spirits soar,
In this whirlwind, we crave more.

Puzzles of Passion and Care

Love's puzzle pieces, scattered wide,
With every touch, the gaps subside.
In laughter shared and whispers low,
Together we craft our vibrant flow.

Every glance a piece of fate,
In tangled paths, we gently wait.
The fire burns with steady grace,
In the puzzle of our embrace.

The Silent Language of Affection

In glances we find, a story to share,
A whisper of love, floating in the air.
The touch of a hand, a gentle embrace,
In these moments, we carve out our space.

Words often fail, but silence can sing,
In the heart's quiet language, love's the real thing.
A smile that ignites, a laughter that glows,
In the silent embrace, true affection flows.

Footprints in the Sand of Time

Each footprint we leave, a tale to unfold,
Imprints of laughter, of sorrow untold.
Shifting with tides, as seasons will change,
The sands of our journey, forever exchange.

In the ebb and the flow, memories play,
Like whispers of time, they fade and they stay.
With every new wave, fresh stories arise,
Footprints in sand, beneath endless skies.

Guardians of the Gentle Flame

In the hearth of our hearts, a flicker resides,
A warmth that ignites, as each moment collides.
Guardians stand firm, with love as their shield,
In the quietest nights, a promise revealed.

With tender devotion, we nurture the light,
A flickering candle, against the dark night.
Together we gather, in this sacred place,
Guardians of love, in its warm embrace.

Paving Stones of Shared Dreams

Each dream we foster, a stone we will lay,
Building a pathway, to light up our way.
With faith in our hearts, we carve out the space,
For the dreams that we share, in this timeless race.

Together we wander, through shadows and sun,
Each step a reminder, two lives become one.
On paving stones bright, in the whispers of night,
We weave our tomorrows, embracing the light.

Harvest Moon of Emotional Bounty

Under the glow of the harvest moon,
Hearts entwined, we find our tune.
Golden fields sway with our dreams,
Night whispers softly, or so it seems.

In the cool breeze, sorrows fade,
Promises linger in the shade.
With every grain that touches ground,
Gratefulness our joy is found.

Laughter dances on the wind,
Together, the light will always send.
Fragrant memories we create,
Holding close what love narrates.

As the moon casts its silver light,
We gather hope, a beacon bright.
In abundance, we share our pain,
Harvesting joy, we rise again.

Bridges Built by Kindness

Across the streams of everyday,
We build bridges in our way.
With every act, a gentle hand,
A world of hope where we all stand.

Through trials faced, we lend our heart,
A bond that's formed, never apart.
Supportive words and smiles shared,
In kindness, we find love declared.

Each bridge a link, we walk anew,
Together facing skies so blue.
With laughter as our guiding song,
In unity, we all belong.

In storms of life, we stand so tall,
With every bridge, we will not fall.
For kindness shines, our guiding star,
Connecting souls, no matter how far.

Reflections in the Waters of Love

In tranquil pools where echoes weave,
The heart's soft whispers, we believe.
Love's reflections gently sway,
Guiding our dreams throughout the day.

Beneath the surface, secrets hide,
In ripples where our hopes abide.
Mirrored skies and heartfelt cries,
In each reflection, love never lies.

With every wave, a new embrace,
Together we dance in endless grace.
The water's depth, a soothing balm,
In every heartbeat, love feels calm.

As twilight falls, we hear the sigh,
Reflections shimmer, time slips by.
In the waters where our souls dive,
Love's embrace keeps us alive.

A Winding Stream of Emotions

Through forests lush, the water flows,
A winding stream where nature glows.
Each twist and turn, a tale to tell,
Of joy and sorrow, all melding well.

Beneath the surface, currents race,
A dance of feelings, a warm embrace.
With every bend, the heart expands,
Emotions thrive like shifting sands.

The gentle rush, a calming sound,
In every splash, our hopes are found.
As seasons change and time moves on,
The stream reflects where we belong.

In the quiet moments, we find peace,
A winding journey that will not cease.
With every ripple, memories bloom,
In this stream of emotions, we consume.

Crumpled Notes of Sweet Memories

In the corners lie whispers,
Tucked in pages, worn and frayed,
Faded ink marks heartfelt letters,
Promises made, now bittersweet.

Laughter dances in the margins,
Sketches of our tangled paths,
Sunlit days and moonlit charms,
Paper trails of love and loss.

Woven dreams in fragile sheets,
Time, a thief of tender tales,
Yet in crumpled notes, we keep,
The echoes of our past unveiled.

With each crease, a moment lives,
Ink reveals what hearts once felt,
In these notes, the love still gives,
Memories like stars, forever spelt.

Blossoms of Longing and Light

Petals drift on summer's breeze,
Whispers of a love that glows,
In twilight's haze, the heart's at ease,
While gentle beams of moonlight flow.

Amidst the gardens of desire,
Fragrant blooms evoke the past,
Yearning hearts in sweet attire,
In their dance, a spell is cast.

Chasing shadows, dreams take flight,
Through the night, our spirits soar,
In every blossom, pure delight,
Awakens what we can't ignore.

With every season, hope ignites,
Longing wrapped in silken threads,
In the warmth of morning's lights,
We find the words left unsaid.

Serenades for Two

Under stars, our whispers blend,
Soft melodies intertwine,
Every note a heart to mend,
In this moment, love we find.

Gentle strumming of guitar,
Captures dreams within the air,
With each chord, we wander far,
Lost in rhythms, unaware.

Laughter twirls like evening mist,
In the quiet, souls embrace,
Every glance, a tender kiss,
Time suspended in this space.

In these serenades, we sing,
Voices rise like morning dew,
In the harmony we bring,
We find ourselves, just me and you.

The Seasons of Our Souls

Springtime whispers through the trees,
Awakening the dormant dreams,
In every breeze, a soothing tease,
Life returns in vibrant streams.

Summer blooms with passion's fire,
Golden rays on love's embrace,
Every heartbeat, a sweet desire,
In warmth, we find our special place.

Autumn casts a glowing hue,
Leaves of amber gently fall,
In the quiet, we renew,
Harvesting the love of all.

Winter's chill, a spark ignites,
In the stillness, hearts stay close,
Through the cold, we find the lights,
Seasons pass, but love is prose.

Echoing Laughter Under Stars

Beneath a sky so vast and bright,
We share our dreams, igniting night.
Laughter dances on the breeze,
Echoing through the ancient trees.

Moonlight bathes our hopeful hearts,
In whispered words, love never parts.
Stars above, a guiding light,
Chasing shadows, embracing night.

With every twinkle, stories told,
In memories warm, our hands we hold.
Together, under velvet skies,
We find the truths that never die.

In laughter's echo, we shall stay,
Filling the dark with joy's array.
Beneath the stars, our spirits soar,
Forever bound, forevermore.

Constellations of Togetherness

In the night, each star's embrace,
Reflects your love, your gentle grace.
Constellations guide our way,
Together, we shall never stray.

In every touch, a spark ignites,
Creating warmth on chilly nights.
Mapping dreams with whispered hopes,
Our journey wide, our hearts elopes.

With every twinkle, wishes made,
A tapestry of love displayed.
In darkened skies, our story's spun,
Two souls entwined, forever one.

Through cosmic dance, we drift and glide,
In constellations, love's great pride.
Together we shine, a radiant pair,
In the universe, we find our share.

A Canvas of Kindred Spirits

Colors blend on life's great stage,
Each stroke a chapter, every page.
Together, we paint our dreams anew,
With every hue, our bond shines through.

The canvas stretches, vast and wide,
In every corner, love won't hide.
We sketch the moments, bright and bold,
A masterpiece that can't be sold.

Through laughter's lines and sorrow's shades,
We weave the threads that time parades.
In every color, a story glows,
Kindred spirits, as our heart flows.

With paintbrush held, we dare to dream,
On this canvas, life's vibrant scheme.
Forever linked in art, we stand,
Creating magic, hand in hand.

Labyrinth of Longing

In the maze where shadows dwell,
I wander lost, hard to quell.
Each turn reveals a whispered plea,
A longing heart, yearning to be free.

The path is twisted, filled with dread,
Yet hope is woven through the thread.
I trace the walls with cautious hands,
In search of love, where silence stands.

Each corner hides a memory,
A flicker of what used to be.
In the labyrinth, my heart will roam,
Seeking solace, a way back home.

Though the journey may feel long,
In every step, I find my song.
Through the corridors of endless night,
I seek the dawn, embracing light.

The Compass of Affection

In the map of our hearts, love finds its way,
Through a journey of whispers, where hopes gently lay.
With the compass of trust, we navigate fate,
A bond forged in moments, never too late.

Every glance is a sign, every touch a guide,
In the storms of uncertainty, together we bide.
With laughter and tears, our path carved in light,
In the compass of affection, everything feels right.

Blossoms of a Gentle Heart

In the garden of dreams, soft petals unfold,
Each blossom a story, a memory told.
With fragrance of kindness, they sway in the breeze,
Whispers of comfort, a sweet heart's ease.

Through the seasons of life, their colors remain,
Painting love's canvas, through joy and through pain.
In the warmth of connection, they flourish and grow,
Blossoms of a gentle heart, a radiant glow.

Navigating the Labyrinth of Souls

In the maze of emotions, we wander and roam,
Seeking the pathways that lead us back home.
With courage as lanterns, we journey ahead,
Guided by love, where our hearts gently tread.

Each twist and each turn, a lesson we learn,
In the depths of connection, our spirits discern.
Through shadows and light, our souls intertwine,
Navigating the labyrinth, your heart next to mine.

Echoes of Eternal Devotion

In the silence of night, our promises ring,
Echoes of love, in the stillness they cling.
With each heartbeat, a vow, steadfast and true,
In the essence of forever, it's me and it's you.

Through the tides of existence, we dance and we sway,
With echoes of devotion, lighting our way.
In the rhythm of time, our love won't depart,
For in every echo, resides a true heart.

Currents of Compassionate Understanding

In the depths of silent seas,
Echoes of hearts begin to merge.
Waves of kindness touch the shore,
As empathy starts to surge.

Through the storms of human plight,
Hands reach out to hold the frail.
Voices rise like whispers soft,
Together we shall prevail.

Each tear shared becomes a bridge,
Offering warmth in the cold.
United in a gentle bond,
Stories of love unfold.

In this dance of light and dark,
We learn to see through each eye.
Currents flow with understanding,
As we let compassion fly.

The Journey Beyond the Horizon

Beneath the canopy of stars,
Dreams are woven, threads of gold.
With each step, the path unfolds,
A tale of courage to be told.

Mountains rise and valleys bend,
Challenges shape our way.
With a heart both bold and true,
We embrace the night and day.

Whispers guide us through the fog,
As the world begins to stir.
With every stride, we paint the skies,
Wandering where hope occurs.

Beyond each twist and turn we take,
Lies the promise of the dawn.
The horizon calls our spirit forth,
To brighten where we've drawn.

Guiding Stars in the Heart

In the canvas of the night,
Stars are scattered far and wide.
Each twinkle holds a tale untold,
In celestial dreams, we confide.

With each wish upon a star,
Hearts ignite with ancient lore.
Guiding lights that steer the soul,
Through darkened paths and open doors.

When shadows whisper doubt and fear,
A spark within begins to grow.
Stars remind us we are not alone,
In the journey, love will flow.

In the quiet of the evening calm,
We find our strength, our place to start.
For in the vastness up above,
Lie the guiding stars in the heart.

Steps Beneath the Moonlight

Amidst the glow of silver beams,
Footsteps dance on paths of dreams.
In the hush of night's embrace,
Whispers echo, hearts race.

Each step holds a story sweet,
As shadows weave beneath our feet.
Moonlit paths invite us near,
To face our joys, to hold our fear.

The world transforms in softer light,
Imagination takes its flight.
Wherever the journey leads us far,
We find our peace beneath a star.

With every stride on this fair ground,
Hope and love together found.
In the stillness of the night,
We walk in grace, our spirits bright.

Threads of Gold weaving Stories

In the silence of the night,
Threads of gold begin to shine.
Weaving tales of old and bright,
Whispers wrapped in gentle twine.

Memories stitch through time and space,
Each loop a moment held so dear.
Stories dance with grace and pace,
In the loom where dreams appear.

Hands that craft with love anew,
Sewing pieces of the past.
Every stitch a bond so true,
Binding hearts that hold steadfast.

As the tapestry unfolds,
Threads reveal their sacred glow.
In the stories each heart holds,
We find the strength to grow.

Petals Falling on Quiet Paths

Petals drifting on the breeze,
Softly landing where they may.
Nature's whispers, sweet and clear,
Coloring the world at play.

Along the paths where silence reigns,
Footsteps echo of the past.
Each flower tells of joy and pain,
Echoes that forever last.

Falling gently, stories weave,
Bright confessions in the sun.
Nature beckons, hearts believe,
In the beauty all can run.

On these quiet, winding ways,
Life unfurls with every breath.
Petals fall, in soft arrays,
Reminding us of love's depth.

Gifts of Time and Tenderness

Time unwraps its gentle gifts,
Moments shared in tender care.
Every heartbeat softly lifts,
The weight of joy, beyond compare.

In the stillness of the night,
Tender whispers find their song.
Wrapped in warmth, the world feels right,
Holding close where we belong.

Each second, a precious gift,
Framed in smiles and laughter's glow.
Through the storms, our spirits drift,
Hand in hand, together grow.

Gifts of time, so soft, profound,
In their presence, joy ignites.
Tenderness in love is found,
Guiding us to endless heights.

Tapestry of Heartfelt Journeys

In the weave of life's embrace,
Tapestries of hearts unveil.
Journeys shared in every space,
Each thread whispers a new tale.

Adventures crafted side by side,
Laughter woven in the seams.
Through the storms, our spirits glide,
Painting pictures from our dreams.

Every journey, rich and bold,
Layers build from love and pain.
As we wander, stories told,
Ties of friendship will remain.

In this tapestry of light,
We find solace, strength, and peace.
Heartfelt journeys feel so right,
In our hearts, the love won't cease.

Celestial Alignments of Affection

In twilight's embrace, stars ignite,
Hearts entwined in soft lunar light.
Galaxies whisper a tender tune,
As dreams soar high, like balloons in June.

With each heartbeat, the cosmos sighs,
Drawing together the wandering skies.
Love's gravity pulls us ever near,
In the dance of fate, no room for fear.

Nebulas bloom in the shades of dusk,
Our spirits soar, as love's sweet musk.
In every constellation, a spark,
Our souls align, forever remarked.

When night falls, we'll trace the divine,
Each twinkle a promise, yours and mine.
With celestial maps, we'll navigate,
The universe sings of our fate.

Resonance of Kindred Spirits

In silent corners, souls converge,
Echoes of laughter begin to surge.
Bound by threads of fate's gentle lace,
Kindred spirits find their place.

With every glance, a spark ignites,
Illuminating the darkest nights.
In shared stories, we weave a tune,
Resonating beneath the moon.

Hearts in rhythm, a timeless dance,
Creating a bond born from chance.
In tranquil moments, we truly see,
The silent whispers of you and me.

Together we stand, unyielding and bold,
A tapestry rich, in stories told.
In every heartbeat, our truth is found,
In the resonance, forever bound.

Carvings on the Bark of Time

Each groove tells tales from days long past,
Moments frozen, memories cast.
Whispers of lovers, laughter and tears,
Etched in the wood through countless years.

Branches stretching, reaching for skies,
Carved not with ink, but with heartfelt sighs.
From tender embraces to joyous glee,
Nature holds witness to you and me.

Seasons change, but the stories stay,
In the rings of life, we find our way.
Each notch a memory, each scar a sign,
Symbols of love on the bark of time.

In every crevice, the echoes remain,
Unraveling the joy, the sorrows, the pain.
Together we weather, against nature's climb,
Living forever in carvings of time.

Thresholds of New Beginnings

At dawn's first light, hope takes its flight,
Each new horizon ignites the night.
With courage in hand, we stand at the door,
Ready to venture, to seek and explore.

Leaves unfurl as the world awakens,
The past behind us, no chains, no fakeness.
In the whispers of wind, a fresh refrain,
Unlocking the joy, releasing the pain.

With every heartbeat, a promise we make,
Towards the unknown, no fear of a break.
In life's tapestry, we find our thread,
Embracing the path that lies ahead.

Together we leap, off the edge we fall,
In the dance of life, we hear the call.
Thresholds of promise, new stories to spin,
In the journey ahead, our hearts will begin.

Conversations Beneath the Moon

In whispering night, we share our dreams,
The silver light weaves soft, bright beams.
Questions dance like shadows on the ground,
In secrets held, our hearts are found.

With each soft sigh, the world slips away,
Under the stars, we let thoughts play.
The moon our witness, serene and grand,
In this stillness, we make our stand.

Words like petals, fall gently down,
In quiet laughter, we wear our crown.
Through every silence, our spirits twine,
In moments shared, your heart is mine.

So let us linger, this night is ours,
Beneath the watchful, twinkling stars.
For in this haven, so pure, so soon,
We find our truth, conversations bloom.

The Symphony of Two Rising

In the dawn's light, a melody plays,
Two hearts entwined in a tender gaze.
Every note a promise, fresh and bright,
We chase the sun, embracing the light.

With every heartbeat, the rhythm grows,
A symphony formed where our spirit flows.
Together we rise, hand in hand,
A dance of two souls, perfectly planned.

The world awakens to our sweet song,
In harmony's embrace, we belong.
Each moment cherished, a fleeting dream,
In life's grand concert, we are the theme.

So let the music of love resound,
A beautiful journey, unbound, profound.
In the chorus of life, we take our cue,
With love as our guide, we'll break on through.

Hidden Gems Within Reach

In quiet corners of forgotten streets,
Treasures lie waiting where the heart beats.
A smile from a stranger, a soft hello,
In simple moments, our spirits grow.

Among the shadows, the sunlight gleams,
Whispers of hope wrapped in our dreams.
Hidden gems shine in the soft embrace,
Of love, of kindness, in every place.

A child's laughter, a fleeting glance,
Life's little wonders invite us to dance.
In mundane paths, through joy and strife,
We find the jewels that adorn our life.

So let us wander, open our eyes,
Discover the beauty beneath the skies.
For in each heartbeat, the truth will teach,
The hidden gems are always within reach.

The Art of Nurturing Souls

With gentle words, we plant the seeds,
In the garden of hearts, we tend to needs.
A touch of warmth, a listening ear,
In this sacred space, our love is clear.

Through storms and shadows, we stand as one,
In life's rough seas, we are never done.
The art of nurturing, a delicate hand,
Creating a world where our dreams can stand.

Every heartbeat shared, a story told,
In tender moments, our futures unfold.
With laughter and love, we gather close,
In this embrace, our spirits engross.

So let us foster, with care and grace,
A tapestry woven in life's embrace.
For in nurturing souls, we find our role,
In the art of love, we become whole.

Serendipity in Soft Glances

In the morning light so fine,
Eyes meet, a spark divine.
Whispers dance upon the air,
Moments linger, hearts laid bare.

Chance encounters, smiles so sweet,
In silence, two souls discreet.
Every glance, a story told,
Serendipity, a joy to hold.

Fleeting touches, warm embrace,
In the chaos, find your place.
Time stands still, the world a blur,
In those glances, hearts confer.

Like soft petals in the breeze,
The universe conspires with ease.
In serendipity, we trust,
Two hearts bind in gentle lust.

The Map of Souls Entwined

Upon this parchment, lines are drawn,
Paths of heart, from dusk till dawn.
Every twist a tale unfolds,
In the silence, love beholds.

Two souls wandering through the night,
Guided by the starry light.
In every step, a memory made,
In the dance of fate, unafraid.

Markers of where we've been,
In the shadows, dreams unseen.
Threads of destiny entwined,
In the fabric, love defined.

With every heartbeat, maps align,
In the journey, your hand in mine.
Together, we navigate the way,
In this life, come what may.

Heartbeats in Harmony

In the stillness of the night,
Two hearts pulse, a sweet delight.
Beats align in perfect time,
A silent song, a subtle rhyme.

Side by side, our breaths entwine,
A melody so soft, divine.
In the rhythm, we find our song,
In each heartbeat, where we belong.

Tuned together, a symphony,
In every glance, serenity.
As shadows dance upon the wall,
Two heartbeats rise, and softly fall.

In harmony, our spirits soar,
Each moment cherished, forevermore.
With every pulse, love's echo found,
In this union, we are bound.

Navigating the Garden of Dreams

In a garden where dreams bloom,
Petals whisper, dispelling gloom.
Every path a secret leads,
In the stillness, heart's true needs.

Beneath the stars, shadows play,
Wandering souls lose their way.
In every flower, a wish takes flight,
Guided by the soft moonlight.

Embracing colors, rich and bright,
In this haven, everything feels right.
Among the blooms, our thoughts collide,
In this garden, we confide.

With every step, the magic gleams,
Navigating through our dreams.
Hand in hand, we explore the night,
In the garden, hearts take flight.

Heartstrings Tied with Trust

In the quiet night we share,
Whispers carried on the breeze,
Entwined hearts made a solemn vow,
Holding tight, we find our ease.

Where dreams are stitched with threads of gold,
Each secret shared is a treasure,
In this safe space, we grow bold,
Trust ignites our truest measure.

With every laugh, a bond is sewn,
Through storms, we'll weather, side by side,
Two souls united, never alone,
In trust, we take the sweetest ride.

Hand in hand, we brave the night,
These heartstrings play a melody,
In every echo, pure delight,
Love's symphony, our harmony.

Melodies of Mutual Respect

In the quiet hum of morning light,
We find a rhythm, soft and true,
Each note reflects a shared insight,
In harmony, we weave what's new.

Your voice, a song, I never tire,
Notes reverberate through the air,
Respecting dreams that never tire,
Together, we create our prayer.

With every step, our dance takes flight,
A balance built on gentle grace,
In every glance, a spark ignites,
We cherish this timeless embrace.

Melodies rise, our spirits soar,
Two hearts entwined in sweet refrain,
United, we'll continue to explore,
In mutual respect, we remain.

Echoes of What Could Be

In the twilight, shadows play,
Whispers of what lies ahead,
Each moment hints at bright displays,
Futures woven in threads of red.

Echoes linger in the air,
Stories yet to be unveiled,
Every glance a silent prayer,
In this space, we're unassailed.

Paths entwined like stars above,
Infinite possibilities,
Guided by the stars of love,
Charting courses through the breeze.

With every heartbeat, dreams will be,
Adventures waiting to be found,
In echoes of what could be,
A canvas where hope abounds.

The Dance of Two Souls

In the moonlight's soft embrace,
We step lightly, hearts in sync,
Each movement flows, a flowing grace,
In this dance, we never blink.

Spinning gently, time stands still,
Two souls gliding, fate aligned,
With every twirl, a budding thrill,
A unity that's rare to find.

With each breath, our spirits rise,
Through this rhythm, we discover,
In every step, a love that ties,
The dance of souls, like no other.

Together we paint the night sky,
With starlit dreams, we forge a path,
In the dance, we never say goodbye,
For love's embrace ignites our laugh.

The Symphony of Us

In the quiet of the night, we play,
Notes of laughter, echoes sway.
Harmony in every glance,
Together we take our chance.

In this melody, hearts align,
With every beat, your hand in mine.
Rhythms dance within our souls,
Creating joy as the music rolls.

Through the storms that come our way,
Our symphony will never fray.
With each challenge, we will rise,
Crafting love beneath the skies.

As the final note drifts away,
Our hearts will linger, come what may.
In the silence, love will stay,
A symphony that will not sway.

Threads of Destiny Interwoven

In a tapestry brightly spun,
Threads of fate have just begun.
Each stitch a story, rich and true,
Interwoven, me and you.

With colors bold, and shades of past,
Our journeys tangled, steadfast.
Through every twist, we find our way,
Together stronger, day by day.

In this pattern, pain may seam,
Yet through the dark, we dare to dream.
Life's loom is fierce, but so are we,
Bound by love, we shall be free.

As threads unite, we weave a goal,
An endless bond that makes us whole.
In destiny's grand, vibrant show,
We find our strength in love's soft glow.

Evening Breeze of Understanding

As the sun dips low, shadows creep,
In the twilight, secrets sweep.
Whispers ride the gentle wind,
An understanding built within.

With every breeze, a soft caress,
Bringing comfort, easing stress.
Silent words, a timeless grace,
In your eyes, I find my place.

Through the night, let silence reign,
In the stillness, feel the gain.
Hearts attuned, no need for sound,
In this peace, our love is found.

As stars awaken, skies embrace,
In evening's calm, we find our space.
With every breath, a shared delight,
Together, we greet the night.

The Lantern's Glow in the Dark

In the night's embrace, shadows play,
A lantern glows, lighting the way.
With flickering flames, it softly calls,
Guiding lost souls through night's thralls.

Each spark a wish, every flicker hope,
Through darkest times, we learn to cope.
With gentle light, our fears subside,
In this warmth, we shall abide.

As the winds howling seem so near,
The lantern's glow wipes away fear.
Through the storms of life we steer,
Together, love will reappear.

In the dawn, when shadows part,
We'll gather light to warm the heart.
With memories bright, we'll leave a mark,
Forever, the lantern in the dark.

The Orchard of Shared Dreams

In an orchard of dreams we stand,
Where whispers dance on twinkling leaves.
Branches heavy, hearts expand,
Among the fruit of all we believe.

Sunlight filters through the trees,
Casting shadows soft and light.
In this place, our souls feel free,
Each moment sparkles, pure delight.

With laughter ringing, voices blend,
In a symphony of trust and care.
We gather hopes that never end,
In each other's hearts, we share.

Together, we will nurture dreams,
Planting seeds for futures bright.
In this orchard, love redeems,
Together we will reach new heights.

Hopes Carried on Gentle Breezes

Hopes sail softly on the breeze,
Guiding hearts to distant shores.
With whispers carried through the trees,
Dreams unfold, opening doors.

Each gust revitalizes our view,
Painting skies with vibrant hues.
In every breath, a chance anew,
To chase the paths our spirit chooses.

We stand as one, hands intertwined,
With faith wrapped tightly 'round our souls.
Through storms of doubt, we stay aligned,
As the winds of fate take their tolls.

On this journey, we will glide,
Trusting the currents of the air.
With love and hope as our guide,
We'll navigate to places rare.

Mornings Woven with Affection

In gentle sunlight, mornings break,
Woven threads of warmth and care.
Each cup shared, a quiet take,
Moments rich, beyond compare.

Songs of birds fill up the air,
A melody of soft embrace.
Together, we find solace there,
In this cherished, sacred space.

With smiles that shine like early rays,
And laughter flowing like a stream,
We cherish these simple days,
Where love is real and hearts redeem.

From morning light to evening's bliss,
We weave our dreams with every kiss.
In the fabric of our days,
Affection blooms in countless ways.

Sounds of Serenity and Warmth

The sounds of nature softly play,
A lullaby for weary hearts.
In whispers, peace finds its way,
Where calm and comfort never part.

Rustling leaves and distant streams,
Together sing a soothing tune.
In these moments, we find dreams,
Beneath the watchful silver moon.

Echoes of laughter fill the air,
As joy and warmth envelop all.
In shared serenity, we care,
Together rise, together fall.

With every sound, our spirits climb,
A harmony of love and grace.
In this refuge, we find time,
Sounds of warmth, a sweet embrace.

Shadows of Truth and Trust

In whispers soft, the shadows play,
Secrets dance in light of day.
Trust we weave like threads of gold,
Truth in silence, stories told.

Beneath the surface, darkness brews,
Yet in our hearts, the light breaks through.
With every step, we learn to find,
A deeper bond that ties our minds.

The echoes linger, memories fade,
Yet steadfast remains the truths conveyed.
In every heartbeat, trust's embrace,
In shadowed moments, we find our place.

Together we stand, side by side,
In the light, where secrets hide.
For in the shadows, truth shall gleam,
A world built strong, a shared dream.

Dancing Flames of Desire

In the night, the embers glow,
Desires rise, like whispers low.
With every spark, our spirits leap,
In fiery depths, the passions creep.

A dance of flames, wild and free,
Unraveled hearts in perfect harmony.
We chase the light, with eyes alight,
Lost in the warmth, we ignite the night.

Each flicker tells a tale untold,
Of longing dreams and love so bold.
Together we burn, a fierce display,
In shadows cast, we'll find our way.

As moonlight wanes, the dawn will break,
But in our hearts, the fire will wake.
For flames may fade, but embers stay,
In the dance of desire, we find our way.

Timeless Threads of Connection

In quiet threads, our stories weave,
A tapestry of all we believe.
Each color bright, a different hue,
Intertwined paths, both old and new.

From distant lands, our spirits meet,
With every heartbeat, connections sweet.
Through laughter shared and sorrows worn,
In every bond, together reborn.

Time may stretch, but still we find,
The ties that link, forever bind.
A circle formed, a sacred space,
In every moment, we find our place.

With threads of love, we stitch the seams,
In the fabric of our wildest dreams.
Together, we'll traverse the night,
For in connection, we find the light.

Beyond the Horizon of Hearts

Where skies embrace the sun's warm light,
Beyond the hills, our dreams take flight.
With every heartbeat, hopes arise,
Towards the unknown, beneath vast skies.

In whispers soft, we chart the way,
Through valleys deep, we'll bravely sway.
Beyond the horizon, loved ones call,
In every stumble, we rise, we fall.

The journey long, the paths may stray,
Yet in our hearts, we'll find our way.
With open arms, we seek to touch,
The beauty found in love, so much.

Together we'll soar, through every part,
For love is the compass of every heart.
With every sunset, a new dawn starts,
In unity, we'll mend our hearts.

Reflections in a Still Pond

The water lays like glass,
Mirroring the thoughts we keep.
Whispers of the past arise,
In the silence, secrets seep.

Gentle ripples brush the edge,
Each ripple tells a story told.
Brightening the shadows cast,
Through memories, brave and bold.

Moonlight dances on the waves,
While stars twinkle far above.
Nature's breath, a peaceful pause,
In this stillness, find the love.

Deep within the liquid calm,
Truth resides in every glance.
Reflections tell of who we are,
Inviting us to take a chance.

Heartstrings and Glowing Maps

In twilight's embrace we meet,
Heartstrings pull where paths align.
Each glance ignites a spark anew,
Guiding us through night's design.

Maps drawn in the stars above,
Charting journeys yet to trace.
Every beat a compass point,
Leading us to love's warm place.

With every laugh and whispered dream,
Threads of fate weave close and tight.
Colors bloom as spirits soar,
In the tapestry of night.

Together we will explore,
The landscapes of our gentle hearts.
In this vastness, hand in hand,
Creating worlds where love imparts.

Harvesting the Fruits of Kindness

In gardens where the soft winds blow,
Seeds of care begin to grow.
With every smile, we plant a dream,
In kindness' soil, hearts gleam.

Hands reaching out, collecting grace,
Gathering joy in every space.
Fruits of laughter, love, and peace,
Harvesting hope that will never cease.

In the bounty of our days,
Compassion lights our gentle ways.
Each act a testament to share,
A simple gesture proves we care.

When we sow with open hearts,
Together we can mend the parts.
Creating ties that bind us close,
In the orchard of love, we can boast.

A Tapestry Woven with Intent

Threads intertwine, colors blend,
Each strand tells a story, my friend.
Crafted gently, stitch by stitch,
In every pattern, we find our niche.

Moments captured, woven tight,
In the loom of day and night.
Intentions clear, designs refined,
In this creation, peace we find.

Emotions dance, a vibrant hue,
Every choice reflects in view.
From joy to sorrow, life's embrace,
Creating art in time and space.

As we weave our lives with care,
Let love's essence fill the air.
A tapestry rich, a shared delight,
Together we can shine so bright.

Garden Paths of Intimacy

In a garden lush and green,
Where love blooms and bees hum sweet,
We wander down the shaded paths,
Hand in hand, our hearts in beat.

Petals dance with morning light,
Whispers of secrets shared between,
Every corner holds a dream,
Filling spaces, soft and keen.

The scent of roses fills the air,
Tracing memories as we roam,
Each step a soft commitment,
This garden, forever our home.

Beneath the bowers, sunbeams play,
While laughter brightens every day,
In the silence, our hearts converge,
In this garden, love's sweet urge.

Footprints in the Sand of Time

Upon a shore of golden grains,
We walk where oceans meet the sky,
Footprints left and washed away,
Reminders of moments gone by.

Each wave a gentle kiss on skin,
As tides keep secrets in their flow,
We turn to trace the paths we've walked,
In the ebb and rise, our hearts do glow.

In fleeting shadows cast at dusk,
The sun dips low, the day does sigh,
We gather these soft memories,
Like footprints left, we can't deny.

For as the sands shift with the swell,
Our stories whispered, every shell,
We cherish all we've come to find,
Imprints of love, linked in time.

Raindrops of Revelation

In the hush of falling rain,
Gentle taps on windowpanes,
Each drop a secret from the skies,
Awakening thoughts that dance and wane.

Puddles form like mirrored dreams,
Reflecting what the heart recalls,
In this rhythm, truths unfold,
As nature's song around us calls.

Lightning flashes, brief yet bright,
Illuminating hidden fears,
With every storm that passes by,
We gather strength from all our tears.

So let the raindrops fall with grace,
Each one a lesson we embrace,
In their whispers, wisdom glows,
Revelations in nature's space.

The Bridge Between Us

Between two hearts, a bridge does sway,
Connecting paths, come what may,
With wooden planks that softly creak,
Our love a gentle, steady stay.

Each step we take, in trust we tread,
Amidst the winds that weave and thread,
In shadows cast by evening's glow,
Together forging what lies ahead.

Beneath a sky of stars so bright,
We share our dreams, ignite the night,
For on this bridge, we stand as one,
Two souls entwined, a graceful flight.

Though storms may come and tempests roar,
This bridge will hold forevermore,
In every heartbeat, every sway,
We find our strength, come what may.

Echoes of Affection

In the quiet of the night,
Whispers drift like soft song,
Hearts connect in gentle light,
Where feelings truly belong.

Memories dance on the breeze,
Fleeting moments wrapped in time,
Each heartbeat a sweet reprise,
In love's tender, rhythmic rhyme.

Stars align in the vast dome,
Guiding souls through the strife,
Together, we find our home,
In the echoes of our life.

With every glance, bonds deepen,
A tapestry finely spun,
In this love, we are awakened,
Two hearts beating as one.

Lanterns in the Twilight

As day fades to dusky hue,
Lanterns flicker, dreams arise,
Guiding paths that we pursue,
Underneath the velvet skies.

Soft shadows begin to play,
Echoes of laughter are near,
Embracing night, we lose our way,
Each moment, a memory dear.

In twilight's embrace, we revel,
Stories woven under stars,
With every heartbeat, we travel,
Healing wounds, mending scars.

Together, we light the dark,
In the space between each breath,
Our spirits, a blazing spark,
Uniting love, conquering death.

Journeys of the Tender Soul

Through valleys deep, our footsteps trace,
Wandering hearts on paths unknown,
In every challenge, we find grace,
Together, yet never alone.

Mountains rise, the skies will weep,
Yet in storms, we find our way,
Secrets of the world we keep,
In the twilight, we will stay.

With kindness as our guiding star,
We journey through the darkest night,
No distance can keep us apart,
Bound by hope and love's true light.

Each road taken is a treasure,
Stories written, lives entwined,
In our hearts, we hold the measure,
Of the dreams that we will find.

Embracing the Heart's Compass

In the depths of the soul's core,
A compass turns, guiding true,
Love's whispers beckon for more,
In every heartbeat, I see you.

Through trials, we rise and fall,
Each moment a chance to grow,
With open arms, we heed the call,
In every storm, our love will show.

With courage as our faithful guide,
We navigate the winding roads,
Hand in hand, side by side,
In this journey, love bestows.

So let us chart this endless sea,
With faith as our sturdy mast,
In the heart's embrace, we will be,
Anchored deep, forever steadfast.

Kites Soaring on Gentle Winds

High above the fields we roam,
Colors dancing, hearts at home.
Breezes whisper, skies so wide,
In the laughter, dreams abide.

Chasing shadows, youth takes flight,
Beneath the sun, everything's bright.
Strings of joy, tied hand in hand,
Together we weave, a vibrant band.

As the day begins to fade,
Winds grow soft, evening's cascade.
In each flutter, a story told,
Of love and hope, and dreams of gold.

With each kite that soars on high,
We find our place against the sky.
Here in the moment, time stands still,
Hearts entwined, united will.

Love Among the Petals

In gardens where the blossoms sway,
Soft whispers guide the day.
Colors blend, hearts entwine,
In fragrant blooms, the world does shine.

Among the petals, secrets spill,
Every touch, a gentle thrill.
Sunlight dapples, shadows dance,
In this beauty, we find our chance.

Butterflies flutter, love takes flight,
In the twilight, all feels right.
With gentle hands, we tend and care,
In each embrace, a moment rare.

Together growing, side by side,
In this garden, hearts abide.
Love unfolds, a blossoming art,
In every petal, we find our heart.

Illuminated Pathways to Connection

Through twilight paths, we find our way,
Guided softly by the day.
Lanterns glow, hearts are near,
In the silence, love appears.

Every step, a bond refined,
In each light, our souls aligned.
Whispers carried on the breeze,
In this dance, we find our ease.

With each turn, new sights we share,
In the glow, there's warmth and care.
Together we walk, hand in hand,
In this journey, dreams expand.

As shadows fade and night draws near,
Paths illuminated, free of fear.
In every moment, connection grows,
In the light of love, our journey flows.

Soft Footfalls of Kindred Spirits

In the quiet of the dawn,
Soft footfalls on the lawn.
Kindred spirits, hearts so bright,
Together weaving pure delight.

With every step, a story shared,
Silent whispers, souls laid bare.
Through the forest, side by side,
In our laughter, we confide.

Footprints imprinted on the earth,
Marking moments of joy and mirth.
Hand in hand, we find our way,
Guided by the light of day.

As the sun sets, shadows grow,
In this bond, love's gentle flow.
Soft footfalls linger in the night,
Together still, our spirits take flight.

Journey of Hearts

Two souls meet on winding trails,
With laughter and soft whispers shared.
Through storms and sun, their love prevails,
In every step, their dreams declared.

Hand in hand, they face the night,
With every heartbeat, hope ignites.
They chart a course, a guiding light,
In each other's arms, they find their sights.

Mountains high and rivers wide,
They navigate the bends and turns.
With trust and faith as their true guide,
In love's embrace, their spirit burns.

As seasons change and time moves on,
Their journey grows, it never ends.
In every dawn, in every song,
The path of hearts forever bends.

Whispered Truths in Twilight

In twilight's glow, soft secrets hide,
As shadows dance and silence speaks.
The day surrenders, dreams abide,
In whispered truths, the heart seeks.

Beneath the stars, a world unfolds,
The night unveils what day concealed.
With every glance, a story told,
In quiet moments, love revealed.

A gentle breeze, a sigh of night,
Embraces souls in tender grace.
With every breath, a spark ignites,
In whispered truths, the heart finds place.

As dreams take flight on starlit waves,
Connections formed through love's design.
In twilight's peace, the spirit saves,
The whispered truths that intertwine.

Beneath the Old Oak's Embrace

An ancient oak, a timeless friend,
Its branches cradle hearts anew.
With tales of old that never end,
In shade it offers moments true.

Beneath its boughs, the children play,
With laughter echoing in the air.
As seasons change from spring to gray,
The tree stands tall, a guardian rare.

In autumn's glow, its leaves take flight,
A tapestry of colors bright.
Through winter's chill, its roots hold tight,
A steadfast love, a guiding light.

As time goes on, the years will pass,
Yet memories linger in the calm.
In the old oak's heart, moments amass,
A sanctuary, forever warm.

Lessons Written in Starlight

A canvas spread across the night,
Each star a lesson, bright and bold.
In silence, they share ancient light,
Whispers of wisdom yet untold.

Through cosmic dance, the heavens sing,
Of love and loss, of hope and fear.
Each twinkle holds a fragile ring,
Of truths we learn when stars are near.

In distant realms, our dreams can soar,
Guided by light of ages past.
With every wish, we seek for more,
As starlit paths in shadows cast.

Embrace the night, let lessons flow,
For every star holds tales to try.
In starlight's glow, the heart will grow,
To find its place beneath the sky.

Secrets of the Heart's Odyssey

In shadows deep, we find our way,
Hidden paths where dreams play.
With every echo, hearts align,
In the silence, love will shine.

Whispers linger in the night,
Guiding souls with gentle light.
Through the struggle, through the pain,
A promise blooms like quiet rain.

Each secret held within a sigh,
A fleeting glance, a passing tie.
Our journey carved by fate's soft hand,
Together we will always stand.

Whispers on the Winding Road

Along the path where shadows dance,
Whispers echo, fate's sweet chance.
Turning corners, hearts appear,
In the stillness, we draw near.

The road may twist, the sky may bend,
But in each step, love will mend.
Footprints mark the tales we've spun,
Every journey has begun.

With laughter, tears, we share our fate,
Moments fleeting, never late.
In the breeze, our hopes take flight,
Whispers weaving through the night.

Love's Mosaic of Moments

Fragments shine in colors bright,
Moments captured, pure delight.
Each memory a piece of art,
Together stitched, we won't depart.

In laughter shared and gentle sighs,
The heart reveals where beauty lies.
In every glance, a story told,
A tapestry of love unfolds.

With every watchful, knowing gaze,
Our journey shimmers through the haze.
In the mosaic, we find our place,
Love's sweet portrait, a warm embrace.

Tides of Understanding

The ocean swells with gentle grace,
Waves of thought in constant chase.
In the rhythm, hearts connect,
Understanding blooms, we reflect.

With every ebb, a lesson learned,
In every flow, a love returned.
Through the storm and calm of night,
We find our way to shared delight.

Like tides that rise and fall anew,
Our bond grows strong, a vibrant hue.
In the depths of each shared breath,
We find the pulse that conquers death.